Splitting SCABS

<u>Title Page</u>

Splitting SCABS

Part III of the "Scabs" Series

poetry by
L.Q. Murphy

L.Q. MURPHY ∞ FRESNO, CA

Copyright Page

Splitting Scabs
Copyright © 2022 by L.Q. Murphy. All rights reserved.
Published by L.Q. Murphy
ISBN 979-8-802084-96-0

All rights reserved. No part of this book may be reproduced or used in any manner without express written permission from the copyright holders. Except for use of quotations in a book review.

This is a work of fiction. This book is sold with the understanding that the author and/or illustrator is not providing advice and/or demonstrations to the reading audience. Always seek professional consultation.

Dedication

- For FAMILY...

Table of Contents

Title Page 3

Copyright Page 4

Dedication 5

Table of Contents 7

Acknowledgments 11

Introduction 13

Body (Core Content) 15

Get It? 16

You. She. See. We. 17

Sometimes Rhythm Rumbled 18

In my Insides 19

The Foot I Plant 20

I'm a Pebble... Maybe 21

Who Relates? 22

Withering 23

Just how it is 24

Which Mask 25

Mourning Son 26

Wishing Hard 27

A reference to something. But what? 28

Shoe by Shoe 29

It Looks Bad 30

Scary Eyes 31

Last Sight was I 32

Fallen Deep 33

The big picture of things 34

The Salt Trail 35

About to Choke 36

A Compass for Dreams 37

Blind 38

Me. A little kid who recycled Cans. 39

A Chance 40

The Roots have Grown 41

Hoops of Time 42

Those Loud Pods 43

Kicking the Blankets 44

The Toll 45

Father's Abusing Sin 46

Pills are like this to Me 47

A Heartbeat Away 48

Flaws that Show 49

Battle to the End 50

Ring of Stones 51

From Hat to Shoe 52

The Variables Involved 53

Just a Nut 54

Where is it? 55

The Weight on You 56

My Reluctant Timeline 57

These Walls 58

Damn Gravity 59

My Longest Loan 60

The Wrong Seeds 61

The "Riddle" Show 62

The More I Try 63

Who Am I? 64

My Stomach Problems Persist 65

Author Biography 67

Product Information 69

Afterword 70

Acknowledgments

There are too many to thank, but I would like to thank my friends and family first if I began someplace. They have sacrificed so I can be myself every day.

I am inspired by the people who came from nothing and earned their way to the dominant class of society. By nothing, I mean people who were shoved to the side, doubted, laughed at, bullied, lied to, discriminated against, and judged unfairly-negative by the mass of society. The people I respect are the ones that found a way to climb to the top echelons of society. Here is a list of people who did not let their dire environments hold them to a lower standard of living: Denzel Washington, Oprah Winfrey, Robert L. Johnson, Nipsey Hustle, Malcolm X, J.K. Rowling, Colin Powell, Mike Tyson, Steve Harvey, Floyd Mayweather Jr., Judge Joe Brown, Robert T. Kiyosaki, and Napoleon Hill. They left clues to follow for success. Clues that help to improve their living conditions.

This is what I can relate to. I can respect the people who want to help every person who desires to improve their life. Real-world heroes consider the lives from the lowest classism to the lives in the highest stratosphere of classism. These are the people I tend to acknowledge the most.

And I can not forget to thank the universe and that highest power in the universe that continues to let me live and breathe another day. Thank you.

Introduction

This book aims to remedy the scabs that strike the hearts of many people.

I, the author, used the writings in this book as a form of therapy. Sorrow, regret, bad experiences, strange experiences, sad outcomes, and dysfunctional lifestyle habits fractured my soul. So, I wrote to find solace.

From the advice and persuasion of others, I made these private writings available to you. You will find solace knowing you do not walk those desolate roads alone—those unforgiving jagged, bumpy roads that cut the flesh we use to laugh and smile.

Suppose you, the reader, will allow me to frame this book. In that case, you will immediately realize that the poems listed are not in order of significance. Just as in life, the poetry written in this book is in random order. The poetry I write is abstract and deep in thinking. From my observation, life is abstract. It is in that abstraction that life found meaning.

We are all different, and that can not be more evident than in the imagination we dwell. That is nothing profound but what is deep is our ability to create physically that which first appeared mentally. This collection of poetry is what emerged for me, and now it is your exclusive visual on the scabs that I still attempt to rebuild. Enjoy!

Body (Core Content)

The
FIRST
and
ONLY
Chapter

Get It?

I see down my leg
I see you pee
Let me grab
A
C - U - P

Don't worry
I see you
And now
I'm going to help you get
In the
I - C - U

Don't cross me
Like a shoe string shoe
Or you'll be hanging from a tree
Saying
Shoo string shoo

You. She. See. We.

What do I do
When someone
Wants all of
You?

Pacing in circles
Heart pumps and skips
Forgetting what I do for
She.

Who came first?
The you or the me.
Two sides of the coin that you
See.

Rubbing my temple
I shallow my breath
What is happening to
We.

Sometimes Rhythm Rumbled

It is too much
Sometimes

My head hangs low
My heart is off
Rhythm

Like the rolling
Of the boulder
My foundation
Rumbled

My rib cage implodes
A breath that wheezes
My heart in your stroller
Careful with the pieces

In my Insides

Butterflies
In the blue vein tubes
Whales
In my heart
Sharks
In my brain.
Warfare
In my insides
This indecisive
Splitting pain.

The Foot I Plant

I try new methods
And fondle new potions
My intestines ache
Ocean to ocean

The foot I plant
What will it grow?
The life of mine
What does it know?

I'm a Pebble... Maybe

Maybe
Just maybe
I'm a pebble
Misplaced
On the ocean's shore

Who Relates?

To eyes
Sounds deceive

To touch
Eyes believe

To taste
Smell debates

To the mind
No one relates

<u>Withering</u>

The green leaf withers
I stand
Still here

                                      And to the earth
                                           I wither
                                        Like the leaf
                                    That disappears

The earth
Like the leaf
To the stars
It withers

                                             The stars
                                  Like a man's short time
                         To the everlasting blackness
                                        Withers
                                      Withers away

The cycle of withering
To existence
Like a drop of blood
Drawn from vengeance
It was bound to happen

Just how it is

Some do
Some don't

Some will
Some won't

Which Mask

Twisting my tangled hair
Deciding which mask to wear

Mourning Son

Run and hide
You morning sun

To safely hide
This mourning son

Wishing Hard

Popping pimples
Wishing hard
Not to be noticed
Not to be scarred

A reference to something. But what?

Shaking my leg
A nervous bee

My heart is racing
What do I see?

A reference too
My splitting scab
Spilling genetics
Inside my lab

<u>Shoe by Shoe</u>

Forty pins
Stand in my shoe
How about we
Exchange
Shoe by shoe

It Looks Bad

Dragonflies dice the layers of air
While the
Lily pads hug the pond

A frog croaks
In a lost pond
Where the sun pokes
In the mountain peaks
Right there
Next to
The glistening creaks

I'm washing
My splitting scabs
It looks bad
It looks bad
This forest knows
My soul is sad
But it's not hard to see
Like a broken knee
My soul limps
And limps
And limps on by
Asking why
As I cry

Scary Eyes

Scary eyes
Above the thighs
Up over hills
Above the rise

What you see
Is far from near
Scary eyes
Will reappear

Last Sight was I

Dust rests upon
An old man's eye
Eyesight unusual
Last sight was I.

Fallen Deep

Assist me now
For I have fallen
Fallen deep
Covered in pollen

The big picture of things

How?
In a world
So vast
She did
It last.

Crushing my staples
Paper cutting my skin
The ink draining dry
I'm thinking of sin

When?
Oh just when
Did he slither
To the top?

The hours I labored
The seasons I've toiled
The cars I've wrecked
The joys that spoiled.

Now...
This! What's this?
Here I arrive
At the bottom
Feeding.

They arrive. I rely.
I'm inside with the spy.

The day comes around
Fortunes will be found.

The Salt Trail

Swirling through the mind
Bending pain
Breaking hearts
Down this pot-holed lane

Fifteen years
Fear caps fear
See the salt trail
From my tears

Don't hold me
Don't watch
It hurts
You'll get lost
Trust me first

A spinning world
Dizzy thoughts
Kicking stones
Breaking tones

About to Choke

Do you get it yet?
A flame
The smoke
It's one
You get it?
You're about to choke

A Compass for Dreams

Spin with the world
Ride the rushing
River
Of time
Your dreams need the compass
To stay the line

<u>Blind</u>

                        Woke up wide
                        Could not see
                            No lying
                       I could not see

                          Help me be
                               Eight.
                        The morning
                       Feeling sheets
                 No more the king

           Where is my bling
                Or a string
           I reach and search
             It is a sting

Twelve noon here
Tripping in my hall
Not tall
Timid
If God hears my call

Who took my vision
That was.
It was.
My focus.
My vision.
My heart.
Dirty rugs.

Me. A little kid who recycled Cans.

For me
The wind blows
Waist deep
Garbage can

No cents
Recycle cans
No sense
Only stands

On my bike
For a few bucks
Baseball cards
Aw shucks
I'm short

Hunger time
Desires large
Parking lots
Dodging cars

Aware of value
I missed those boats
Dodging haters
Cold nights in coats

Desperate night
Desperate dreams
Life my fight
Alone
No teams

A Chance

The twilight star
Ends the day
Like a man
With no arms
No reach
No play

A story
A bay
I had the chance
It was there
Just begging
The teasing hair
Like a
Like
A large red ball
Now rolling by the fair

The Roots have Grown

Life twisted and shifted
Offset by sadistic sin
He made a dirt home
The couch crippled him down
Creativity divorced him
Potato roots have grown

Hoops of Time

Kicking through the hoops of time
Rings of smoke
Grab it if you can
No way
No time to joke

This time a world
Not of solid
Not of rock
But We got it

The hoops of time vanish
The more emotion I evoke
The hoops of time manage
To laugh at me as I choke

Those Loud Pods

I talk to the wall
Chattering jaws
Lisp interruptions
My head dips and nods
My shoulders tense
There is corruption in these pods

Kicking the Blankets

Kicking the blankets loose
Clinching the side of beds
I find it
Music on
Scrub my hair

Find those roaches
In the open they move
Performing right now
I think move by move

Clothes rag like
Smell like hell
Cash is the hope
A disgusting tale

Once you have seen my days
And lived my ways
You might understand the joke
That I should've grabbed the rope

The Toll

I can see an equal
Balanced
Covered by the coal
Good with the bad
On this long dusty road
They said they could have paved it
But what would have been the toll?

Father's Abusing Sin

A home vacant on a valley hill
White paint flakes drifted with the breeze
Resting pollen upon the porch made from skill
Trace by trace footsteps led with a tease

Today the home a focus of destruction
No use for a home known for tragedy
No use for a home that spewed destruction
"This is the life of people your majesty"

Mother, father, daughter, and youngest son
Father lashed the mother daughter and only son
A thundering zenith that echoed till went the sun
The mother's only hope for daughter and son laid in a gun

Father caged his only wife, daughter, and son
No love from his father. So... no love given too
It developed from shoe to shoe. From moon to sun
No happiness. No fun. He couldn't run. Sad but true.

The echoes swirled with the summer breeze
The yacking sounds. The hacking sounds. The "no, no," sounds
So sad for boy. So sad for girl. Lacking time. Lacking keys.
Mother poisoned father. He knew she just snatched the crown.

For he was poisoned like a rat. A pesky rat that had to go.
He hid the bullets that day so poison played its role.
Scabs to the three skulls. Karma tickled his big toe.
The vacant valley home... It falls... A needed and grated toll.

Pills are like this to Me

A pill
Filled with the tears
Of a lost curious child
Of the young years

Beneath shades of green
It dropped on his head
A delicately spotted
White
Little egg

To realize that he
Be the cause
Of crash
And of tragedy
Within the spring
Many flower scenes
A possible life
Mixed with shell pieces
And his tears

A winter's scene
In the season of spring
Death on a nice day
A precious life
Never met the day

A Heartbeat Away

My head tilted left
My palm to the artery
I pressed
I prayed

I marched forward
At a machine's pace
Muscles pumping
Heartrate jumping
My pressing pressure

Genetic soup
Seeping between my fingers
Gravity sucking my blood
Below the ground I go
Back to the only universe
I know

Flaws that Show

A black stone
With lines
Lightning white
Tripped me up
Brought me down
The only stone
That was all around

What did it mean?
What was it saying?

Like a stallion
Enraged
It was something
I couldn't hold
It was something
I couldn't hide

A lone stone
On the lone road
A flaw
I need to hide

Battle to the End

Against the opponent's bones
A dense thud
Pop
Crunch
Down
It falls to the mud

Still though.

I won't be
Going home,
But
Neither will he

Neither,
Is...
the cost to be.

Ring of Stones

Within that ring
Holds a tempered soul
Acutely dancing
On bumpy roads

Nine jewels gleam
The son wears the ring
A misplaced jewel
The diamond
On the ring

Son talks
Of the third jewel
Slathered blue
Nearby sits
The emerald greens

He stares at this stone
Hypnotized
He roams
Stones within stones
Passion
He's all alone

I don't expose his thoughts
For fear of his heated skin
If he explodes
The ring will be lost again
And to make again
Will take too many years
With many, many tears
From many, many years.

From Hat to Shoe

You know
If I were you
I'd stop eating
From that shoe

I know
Your stomach churns
I can feel it
I know it burns too

And it turns
Inside of you
Sharp needles
In the guts
Join too

I swallowed
Splinters
Woodchips
Termites followed too
Down
Down
Swallowed
Something else followed too

Scraping my organs
Tearing my skin
Down to my toes too
And every inch of intestine

I can't see these scabs
But I know they form too
From head to toe
Even from hat to shoe

The Variables Involved

I am better than this
But I
Cannot
Escape this stake
My mishaps
My mistakes

I should be aware
But I
Seem to only…
Beware

Count handsomely
The variables involved
Can't you see
How the situation evolved?

Just a Nut

Just a nut
Crushed beneath
Time's massive branch

Just a nut
From one fall
One "Timber" call

Just a nut
The fault of one?
No
It is the fault
Of everyone

Just a nut
With a broken shell
Living a life
In the valleys of Hell

Where is it?

Have you ever seen
A dreamy thing
It seemed unreal
But sadness seemed
To invoice your heart
Requiring
Nothing but
The misery

Of such a day
When you see
A truthful scene
Like a fallen leaf
That starts the chill
Of winter's hell
Love is gone
The devil's bell
Love is gone
An empty well
The thirsty soul
That dug the well

You kept digging
But
Didn't understand
The harder you tried
The more broken the land.

The Weight on You

How heavy
Is the gold?
How heavy
Was the toll?
How many let downs was it
Till you turned cold?

My Reluctant Timeline

You see
I really want it
But I fear
Sometimes
My timeline
Won't own it

These Walls

The white walls
They pinch
They close me in
Next to the brown wood
Where I do my sins

My fingers twitch
Deep in my thoughts
I have an itch
And she's a witch
Who formed a hitch
Now she won't leave
Till my final twitch

Damn Gravity

My blood wants to stay
Damn gravity

I know you want my flesh
Damn gravity

But you're
The one thing I can rely
Damn
Gravity

I sit here in this chair
Because
Damn
Gravity

My food stays on my plate
Because
Damn
Gravity

Truthfully
I want to be with the moon and stars
Damn Gravity

But again
Truthfully
I am not the only one
Fighting this
Damn Gravity

My Longest Loan

The one thing I know
Are the terms
Of this loan

I'll give it back
So, universe
Just relax

I know my credit score
I know that others
Would just
Hit the door
But don't foreclose
Before the time

The Wrong Seeds

You get
What you plant
My mother swore to me
Now I reap
What I sow
And this that I
Sow now
Is what
Grows now
Where the devil
Goes now

I am
Sure now
That I
Planted
The wrong
Seeds now

The "Riddle" Show

I tip my toe
Toe by toe
Now I hear
The "Riddle" Show
They tip-toe too
Like a tiger's toe
Silent like
Voodoo!
So, think quick
What will you do?
When the tiger
Comes for you

The More I Try

The more I try
The more I cry
The more I push
The more
THEY
Push back
The more I lie below
The more they stack above
The more I tell the truth
The more they lie
The more I try to live
The more I seem to die
The higher I climb this cliff
The further I am to fall
The more I eat
The more my guts eat me
The more words I learn
The more I need to learn
The more time I stick around
The more time I wish would stick around
The more I seem to desire
The more pain I seem to encounter
The more I sleep
The more I long to seek
The more I think
The more I wish for a final blink
The more I want to say
The more vomit comes my way
The more I want a happy day
The more disappointment comes my way
The more I give in to my soul
The more I eventually win
The more I flow with things
The more I seem to flow with things

Who Am I?

Near a lava river
Built of Iron
Who am I?

I chop the stones
Rotate the rivers
The mountains moan
Will you try?

A sound that shutters
A sound that shakes
The brains of many
And the souls shake plenty

I am the sandpaper to your ear
I am the glue mixed into your tears
I am the razor in your throat
The needles in your fears

You lost me. I found you.
You made me. I crowned you.
You had me. I fooled you.
Do you know
What kills you?

Get the lemon from your eye
Grab the snails from your hair
Brush the dust from your throat
You think I wanna play fair?

I'm built from iron
Who am I?
You want to play?

My Stomach Problems Persist

My stomach
Ouch
The food
The pouch

A stomach compressed
By broken rocks
It always bothers
Like broken clocks

A balloon of acid
Rests in my throat
Move the wrong way
And up it goes

Saliva collects
In my cheeks
What did I eat?
Will I defeat?

Saliva stop!
I'm feeling weak.

My stomach ouches
The crap I eat
My intestines
They've reached their peak.

The END...

Author Biography

About the Author

Born, in 1983, to an African American family (descendent from slavery) in Salinas, California, Lawrence Murphy Jr. joined the United States Army at age eighteen to become a United States Army Airborne Ranger. During his service, he deployed four times to combat zones: two times in support of Operation Enduring Freedom (the war in Afghanistan, 2001) and two times in support of Operation Iraqi Freedom (the war in Iraq, 2003). After his military service, Lawrence Murphy Jr. pursued studies of business finance at Fresno State University, achieving distinction; earning the graduating status of cum laude. During college, he met his wife. They have two children. Lawrence enjoys reading, writing, studying martial arts, watching movies, and enjoys warm spring afternoons with family and friends.

Follow the author on **social media**:

- Instagram   @lq.murphy
- TikTok   @lqmurphy
- Twitter   @LQ_murphy
- LinkedIn   linkedin.com/in/lawrencemurphyjr

Product Information

"Gift Yourself Insightful, Therapeutic Poetry"

- ***The I in my Eye***
  L.Q. Murphy

  Dark poetry with art ready to help you rethink the world. Intense emotions from the poetry make the mind rethink. Poetry and art help readers learn more about human nature. This book is a mixture of poetic themes. **eBook, paperback, and hardcover**

- ***Broken Scabs***
  L.Q. Murphy

  Offered to you is the immense emotional poetry about the sharp pains of life, similar to a broken scab. Like the scab, we use poetry to heal and become better people. The book contains five themes of life. Each theme section contains poetry written to remedy emotional wounds. Scabs. They can be to either our pity or they can be the opportunity to learn and improve. **eBook, paperback, and hardcover**

- ***Rebuilding Scabs***
  L.Q. Murphy

  Fifty poems written from the healing heart. Immerse yourself in abstract and provocative poetry. You are offered unique mixture of poetry that strives to add values like understanding, forgiveness, and wise perspective. **eBook, paperback, and hardcover**

Afterword

"Thank YOU"

"I am grateful. That is all that I am. I think life waits, basically bored, just waiting for all of us to experience it. Congratulations! You just now did that. And... the universe thanks YOU for that. I, definitely, thank YOU for allowing me to serve YOU."

- *L.Q. MURPHY* *(father, husband, U.S. Army veteran, author)*

Printed in Great Britain
by Amazon